Peregrine Questions

poems by

Colette Anderson Gill

Finishing Line Press
Georgetown, Kentucky

Peregrine Questions

Copyright © 2017 by Colette Anderson Gill
ISBN 978-1-63534-197-3 First Edition
All rights reserved under International and Pan-American Copyright Conventions.
No part of this book may be reproduced in any manner whatsoever without written permission from the publisher, except in the case of brief quotations embodied in critical articles and reviews.

ACKNOWLEDGMENTS

Grateful acknowledgment goes to the editors of the journals and the chapbook in which these poems were first published or are forthcoming, some in earlier versions or with alternate titles:

Connecticut River Review: "A Lesson about Rain from Lourdes" and "In History's Grip"
Finishing Line Press: "Ruth's Body Speaks" appeared in the chapbook *Silk & Sting*
Naugatuck River Review: "Sand Dollars"
Oberon Poetry Magazine: "Family Legacy, a Humbling Perspective"
RHINO: "After-Life: an Imagined Macumba Priestess Explains"
Smartish Pace: "Landscape with Elk & Aspen, 2015"
The Southeast Review: "Courage in a Russian Museum"

Publisher: Leah Maines

Editor: Christen Kincaid

Cover Art: IStockPhoto.com

Author Photo: Thomas J. Gill

Cover Design: Elizabeth Maines McCleavy

Printed in the USA on acid-free paper.
Order online: www.finishinglinepress.com
also available on amazon.com

Author inquiries and mail orders:
Finishing Line Press
P. O. Box 1626
Georgetown, Kentucky 40324
U. S. A.

Table of Contents

Moscow, Pink Jolt, Pushkin 1

A Lesson about Rain from Lourdes 2

Courage in a Russian Museum 4

Ruth's Body Speaks 5

Chatting with Self near Toulouse 6

In History's Grip 7

Uncovering Akhmatova & Petersburg 10

Family Legacy, a Humbling Perspective 11

The Absence of a Place 12

Sand Dollars 13

To Namesake, Sidonie-Gabrielle Colette 16

Thanksgiving Morning 17

After-Life: an Imagined Macumba Priestess Explains 18

Landscape with Elk & Aspen, 2015 19

Notes 22

Additional Acknowledgments 24

for Thomas & James Gill

"Peregrine falcon, so called because the young were not taken from the nest…but were caught on their passage or pilgrimage."
—*The Oxford English Dictionary*

"We live in history the way fish live in water."
—Mark Slouka

Moscow, Pink Jolt, Pushkin
Sheremetyevo Airport

Crammed in like cod and oiled by June's heat,
not a single Russian looks up
when two soldiers tongue-lash and shove
a youth with fuchsia hair.

Is 'Chechnya' stamped on his passport?
I clasp my puce suitcase. Do they detest spiky hair?
I'm all patched-wing sympathy,
jammed in Aeroflot's gates.

Seat belts click. Tea speckles red cushions.
So why does the shov-ee spurt
down the aisle as brisk as a trout
and bob in beside me?

Thrumming to Petersburg, crumbs of his history
sail into my lap. And, I kid you not,
Pushkin's tale of a golden fish,
pulsing with soulfulness.

A Lesson about Rain from Lourdes

She comes in rivulets so we taste
        her mist. Brazil has brewed
a *lavadeira* in plastic shoes

and odors from her coconut
        soap infuse our skin. Lourdes
scrubs our clothes on sideboards

made from coarse porphyry.
        Her scarred knuckles flash
like fronds in evening rain

and as we spot them, chills
        come, as if with sunburn's
blisters; though now it's June

and the rainy season. I slog
        to the open-air laundry:
Uma blusa 'stá pronta, Lourdes?

All is wet, my daughter, she
        sighs, *Todo mojado,* and she
towels her child's cornrows.

Our mother's gone to the States
        for grim treatments. Slippers
no longer graze the parquet.

How do fishing boats go on
        dipping, the master's chalk
spalling off? School friends

furtively check our eyes,
    air-kiss cheeks to whisper,
Todo bem, amiga? A lizard

licks at faith and waiting
    is viscous—a sloping road's
reddish clay slurs down a hill.

How does Lourdes manage
    to starch and press school
fardas into cardboard? They

wilt the instant we crack
    the door. Sweaters reek,
loafers run on bleached socks

and Lourdes' eyes roll.
    She and her *filhos* slosh
up granite steps for *mamão*—

smushy papaya—and *café*.
    She rests on her haunches
during the downpours.

Uma blusa 'stá pronta?-Is a blouse ready?
Todo bem, amiga?-Everything okay, friend?
fardas-uniforms

Courage in a Russian Museum
to poet, Osip (Joseph) Mandelstam

This Fabergé egg: gold encases
blue and rose in rhombus cells

and Joseph's Old Testament coat
enclosed its hues in lavish strips.

You Josephs discovered 'brothers'
purple the throat before the pit.

It was you, shadowed poet, who
murmured, *Names serve as omens*

but fear didn't rend your readings.
Trains plowed you to Vladivostok

in a frayed coat, to gulag camps—
jeweler Stalin's ice and skeleton

cloisonné. No flight or passage.
But you argued, *Words are stones*

so you return, as if from Egypt,
in lines like tones on alexandrite.

Ruth's Body Speaks
>*"Whither thou goest…"*
>—*Widow, Ruth, to her mother-in-law, Naomi.*
>*Ruth 1:16*

The truth is, I had not thought
I would leave with Naomi.
Still, the evening before she
un-hobbled the donkeys,
I loosened clothes and slipped
into slumber. And a man
from Israel entered Moab.
He unraveled floor mats
and seeded night with scents.
His wedding garland: myrtle
twined with yellow roses.
How he stirred up my night
clothes as he surrendered
barley-brown robes. And we
arose as a desert dervish,
a swirling sandy funnel
spinning off little dirt,
but the grit and mizzle of pear
and juicy flesh of apple,
peeled until it shivers.
And from these barren thighs
rushed a son—eyes, dark as dates,
and tufts like spun honey.
So on one whorl, I glimpsed
my grandson fling a stone
at a giant Philistine,
Israel's priests anoint his curls
with sacred oil. Friends,
it was a hope's revival in sleep
and not a scribe's artful story.

Chatting with Self near Toulouse

Caress the hills and air
    carved in pastels,
scents as strong
       as lavender fields.

Forage in your suitcase
       for a camisole,
fine as stitched starfish,
       silken snowflakes,

but don't forget the books,
    you heft
  from every metal
      carousel.

So these weeks aren't
    mesh totes, bursting
with brie,
     brioche and truffles?

No, Epicurus thought,
     'Pleasure is a good,
but don't drown
    in that ocean'

and, Prodigal One,
    if you neglect
native pastures,
    even the sweetest
slice of cantaloupe
    ices sun-warmed plates.

In History's Grip
    for Marina Tsvetaeva

i. Paris and the Return to Moscow

Going gray, her stockings twisted,
thinking outside the lines;
she fights poverty in Paris
and scrawls inspired rhymes.

Should Marina and son return
to landmarks 'Reds' defaced?
Moscow, lit by holy icons,
how many have they razed?

She fastens an amber necklace,
its honey-warmth her shield;
but she will end in Tatarstan,
laid in a muddy field.

Trains to a dacha near Moscow
to join Alya and Sergei.
Daughter and spouse are watched
and soon they're marched away.

ii. Managing in Moscow

Marina finds a grimy flat
but the fires gutter.
Vous! Mur addresses Marina
—no longer calls her, Mother.

She cooks a foraged salmon,
though pink flesh breaks apart
like centers of today's failed states.
Her words seem lost—and art.

Her pen once leapt a table's scars:
"I lean with muscle and wing,
my rivers tilt towards you.
My lips seek yours, like spring."

—Nazis start to bomb the city
folks whisper, *She's a spy.*
Mur scales a gable to shoot.
They've got to leave, he'll die.

iii. Shelter in a Tatarstan Village

So Boris Pasternak helps them
to Kimki for a ship.
(Marina craves release by then,
a nail with magic tip.)

The Tatars whisper, *She's crazy,*
but rent an earthy room.
As Mur's disdain grows dimmer,
thoughts of Sergei in his tomb.

One morning, Mur and peasants
leave at sunrise to pave
the landing field for Stalin's planes—
a loaf-for-work exchange.

The nail for hanging oxen yokes
with rope securely knotted.
They cut her down in an apron,
her notebook shaped the pocket.

Going gray, her stockings twisted
the poet marked her times.
Even as we war in this century,
we can't rub out her lines.

Uncovering Akhmatova & Petersburg
in and near Akhmatova's flat, 2008.

> *"Your lynx-eyes, Asia,*
> *they lure into the light*
> *my buried self..."*
> —Anna Akhmatova

Roofs turn to bluish dunes beside the Neva.
White Nights, we murmur, *June beside the Neva.*

This lacy fan enhanced her dark Tatar looks
and painters swooned beside the Neva.

Our ears improve. *Thanks* is *spasiba*.
A yellow-billed loon croons beside the Neva.

Nikolay, a married lover. Flats were like gold.
His family and she, marooned beside the Neva.

This bench is missing slats. The maples tremble
like veterans hawking spoons beside the Neva.

Silver Age poets rocked The Stray Dog—
ghosts in a cellar saloon beside the Neva.

Women froze here outside Kresty Prison.
Few parents were immune beside the Neva.

Mariinsky Theatre's toe-shoe evening.
Hairpins are tiny harpoons beside the Neva.

Symbolist to Acmeist. Paradigms shifted.
Poets' revolution á la Kuhn beside the Neva.

Anna's fame grew. Stalin barked, *Reel in her son*
and guilt shadowed noon beside the Neva.

Surrender self-pity—that red cowberry bush
Russians don't water or prune beside the Neva.

Tonight, tycoons slurp caviar. Granite shimmers.
Sailors pull in gill nets, cocoon beside the Neva.

Family Legacy, a Humbling Perspective
to Lev, Anna Akhmatova's son

It's movie night. Forget about the price.
Your parents are your ticket to the show
so bribe or barter, pay in fur or spice.

The velvet smells old. You whisper in line:
A grandma raised me near Tsarskoe Selo.
It's movie night. Forget about the price.

You buy some wine. It costs you twice.
My father shot—crimson roe fell on snow
—no bribe or barter paid in fur or spice.

In darkness light-motes skip by like dice.
My bed at Anna's? A trunk by the stove.
It's movie night. Forget about the price.

Do you wallet the pass or shred it like rice?
Her poems bring me guards—bunks in rows—
no bribe or barter paid in fur or spice.

The frigid gulags breed a taste for knives,
but you knead and knuckle books like dough.
It's movie night. Forget about the price
and bribe or barter, pay in fur or spice.

The Absence of a Place
    "*The hills look like white elephants, she said.*"
    —Ernest Hemingway

Ernest painted, what? A couple
shadowboxing in Spain
around the word, 'abortion,'

but in the writer's life,
though he craved a daughter,
Greg, the third son, came.

Ernest, wife and elder sons
fished or skied—left Greg
with the maid's one-ton tongue.

Some babes ice-chute to exile.
In a case I know,
the newborn's *labia majora,*

like a deep-notched apricot,
spawned a long silence.
Three daughters. No sons.

"Spoiler" and "No place"
blossomed mute and orange
as zucchini flowers. Are

those the words the Moors
carried to white domed houses
in Málaga—and émigrés

weigh now as they plate
their last dates
for long-rooted neighbors?

Sand Dollars

i.
It was the hot and windy tropics.
It was the true and traitorous thoughts.
Or was it the inkling my parents
needed a new honeymoon?

This in Salvador, Brazil
as the U.S. colluded in a coming coup—
and friends and I twisted to the Beatles'
Love, love me, do.

My mother scoured a leaflet about Rio
I gave her, though she felt sick,
and eyes like farm minks, wavered.
Did they picture a new swimsuit?

We can't afford it, she snapped.
The stylus jigged to its vinyl track.
But is memory a crumbling sidewalk,
tiled in black and white?

My family had sailed south
as Brazil's president tacked left,
and now the generals buzzed like wasps,
as if in a mythic cave.

Still, I think the ex-pats saw my parents
as 'platinum' when Father, a firefly,
switched on his chemistry.
Textbooks and pools with palms shone

'till one day at Barra Beach.
Father swam and Mother breathed,
Just don't marry beneath you
and my stomach dove like a thief's.

But what if intrigues hadn't
undermined *Presidente* Goulart
and this couple, too?
What if they had tasted Rio?

ii.
Suppose in that hive of culture,
slums and régime buzz,
my folks had eaten avocadoes,
stuffed with pink lobster?

What if she'd slipped her English
hips into naked-toed sambas,
or clutching Sugar Loaf's gondola,
his eyes had conveyed a poem?

Suppose they had pried
the hurt and subversion
from their hearts, like small
ocean snails' suction feet?

What if they had whispered
a pact to work in concert
under the towering Christ's
open hands?

But no, Brazil and I
would lose our votes.
Mother flew to a California
healer, she worshipped.

Father needed cover
to court Bianca, my teacher:
*Come with us to a night club,
to Lighthouse Beach, to...*

I could've said No to spaces,
blurred as evenings on a lake
and kept my tote of sand dollars,
clean and tapered as trust.

But after the coup, Father
flew home to witness his wife pass,
and my heel ground the dollars
into pale dust.

To Namesake, Sidonie-Gabrielle Colette
"Nothing is in the intellect that was not first in the senses."
a cottage near Saint-Tropez

You sweep up fallen apples and smell
of thyme and furry sage. As the hose

engulfs the flutes on acorn squash,
a fountain pen scrapes on woven paper

flooding furrows. You scratch the cat
with coiled tail and scribble for hours,

but your kohl-lined eyes haunt the duvet.
Maurice, a younger pearl broker, warms

and twists the sheets. *Vin* tints a goblet,
wicks flame. Glass paperweights flush

like currants. Fifty years old. (Don't fib!)
Didn't the Belle Époque and the Great War

fade before your flashy Paris carousel?
Two husbands, gay lovers, nude scandals

so your novels oozed like berry crepes.
But this autumn, you find the *axis mundi*:

your pen, the soil, a bright man with verve.
The days wind up neatly as the garden hose.

---

*axis mund*i- the world center, or the
connection between Heaven and Earth

Thanksgiving Morning
   to Thomas

The coffee's steam eases our faces
so I say, *Can't you see our mothers,
Joyce and Mary, chatting in space?*
They'd talk of leaving—separation.

Mary would polish her wire-rims:
"Lightning blanched the prairie night.
My son a baby, we rattled home
on tracks and ties and I caught polio…"

As our mothers sip some Earl Gray,
the porcelain teapot's not mittened.
They lean in for warmth and to listen,
as if the words' vowels were missing.

Joyce blurs red lipstick on cup rims:
"Brazil, and that stone in one breast.
A daughter styled and sprayed
my hair before the *Pan Am* left…"

We find the kitchen hasn't moved.
'Seen the celery? —Where is a pie tin?
I lay the pastry tracks across pumpkin.
You bard a pheasant's breast with bacon

while, yes, our shadow mentors mist in:
"More butter!" – "You never put enough."

After-Life: an Imagined Macumba Priestess Explains
Salvador da Bahia, Brazil

She wears a turban, bluish garments flow
and pipe in golden teeth turns accent smoky:

You think the place-beyond will reek of bleach?
Well, naõ, a sugary cocoa fused with salt.

Brazil's aromas, somehow. You still recall
your garden's red loamy breath in Bahia?

That's it: a muddier Eden. Palmy gusts
import a whiff of shrimp from blackened pots,

a muted samba. Strange, naõ? Some spirits
show up in Speedos. Others, hospice smocks.

An earth-bound difference—old geography.
Odors waft from cities you laughed in most.

Cilantro zests red snapper, leafs its oils;
a peeled caju perfumes your snarly roots.

Meus filhos, sink your toes in sand and brine
and drift in like an oyster's tangy salt scents.

Macumba-an Afro-Brazilian religion
caju-fruit in which the cashew grows
meus filhos-my children

Landscape with Elk & Aspen, 2015

Dawn and pine needles scratch
   on the deck's redwood,
"Will this house be my last?"

While my spouse works away,
I wake alone and fingers
   run the bed table's rim.

There's the light dust
      from a red tiled
roof in Caracas,
      spritzed with rain,
kudzu leafing
a New Orleans wall and—

A fox barks. Why
   do houses mist away
like mountain sheep?

The dog and I
   pad downstairs and steer
   by phantoms, sifted
from twenty-two houses:

bar stools, dim as half-moons,
   afghans, draped
      like mountain folds
near keepsakes from Milan,
   La Paz and…

Our Lhasa whines on orange tiles
    from Saltillo,
  Let me out to sniff the world.

The scent—spruce fired in wood stoves—
  and breath spikes, a moment, in air,
    No more wishing, *What if...*
        just this?

This coffee's warmth and white foam,
  this peach's cold meat and stone.

        Traveler,
      fitful ex-pat—
    have you strayed home?

Notes

The book's epigraph by Mark Slouka is from *Nobody's Son: a Memoir*.

"Moscow, Pink Jolt, Pushkin" Alexander Pushkin's tale is "The Fisherman and the Golden Fish" translated by Irina Zheleznova. It is a fairytale about greed.

"Courage in a Russian Museum" is indebted to Gregory Freidin's *A Coat of Many Colors: Osip Mandelstam and His Mythologies of Self-Presentation*.

"In History's Grip" Lines in the ballad which Marina Tsvetaeva wrote are between quotation marks. They were translated by Elaine Feinstein, Angela Livingstone, and Ilya Shambat and were re-arranged to meet the ballad's rhyme requirements. Elaine Feinstein's biography of Tsvetaeva, *A Captive Lion*, provided the circumstances of her final months.

"Uncovering Akhmatova & Petersburg" The epigraph is from the poem "Your Lynx Eyes, Asia…" found in *Poems of Akhmatova* translated by Stanley Kunitz with Max Hayward.

"The Absence of a Place" was partly inspired by, and titled in response to philosopher and activist Simone Weil's imperative, "We must take the feeling of being at home into exile. We must be rooted in the absence of a place." from "Decreation."
"Hills Like White Elephants" is from *The Complete Short Stories of Ernest Hemingway*.

"Sand Dollars" In 1964, Brazilian President João Goulart was replaced in a military coup. The coup subjected Brazil to a military regime politically aligned to U. S. interests until 1985.

"To Namesake, Sidonie-Gabrielle Colette" The epigraph is from an axiom which Thomas Aquinas adapted from Aristotle's Peripatetic School of Philosophy. Some details in the poem were taken from *Secrets of the Flesh: A Life of Colette* by Judith Thurman.

Additional Acknowledgments

Gratitude also goes to these journal editors and poetry contest judges:

"A Lesson about Rain from Lourdes" received the *Connecticut River Review's* 2013 Poetry Prize;
"In History's Grip" was awarded second place in *CRR's* 2010 Poetry Contest;
"Ruth's Body Speaks" received second prize in the Newburyport, Massachusetts Art Association Poetry Contest, 2006;
"Landscape with Elk & Aspen" was a finalist in *Smartish Pace's* 2010 Beullah Rose Poetry Contest;
"Courage in a Russian Museum" received Honorable Mention in *The Southeast Review's* Gearhart Poetry Contest, 2013.

A thank you to the Summer Literary Seminars organization for a fellowship to study poetry in St. Petersburg, Russia. I am indebted to poets Rigoberto González and Jacqueline Kolosov. The book has fewer flaws due to their insights.

"After-Life: an Imagined Macumba Priestess Explains" was conceived for fellow-writers, Vernon L. and David A. Anderson, but it is for all my siblings. "Thanksgiving Morning" is dedicated to Julie Anderson Allphin (1945-2016).

Colette Anderson Gill is the author of the poetry chapbook *Silk & Sting*, published by Finishing Line Press. Her poems have appeared in *Connecticut River Review, Tar Wolf Review, The Southeast Review, The Texas Review*, and others. The recipient of the Howard Moss Poetry Award from the University of Houston, she has also worked as a master's-level psychologist and an English instructor to foreign students at Rice University in Houston. She lives with her husband in a cabin in Evergreen, Colorado.

www.ingramcontent.com/pod-product-compliance
Lightning Source LLC
LaVergne TN
LVHW041516070426
835507LV00012B/1623